STEPHEN CURRY

BY BRETT SMITH

SportsZone

An Imprint of Abdo Publishing
abdopublishing.com

abdopublishing.com

Published by Abdo Publishing, a division of ABDO, PO Box 398166, Minneapolis, Minnesota 55439. Copyright © 2018 by Abdo Consulting Group, Inc. International copyrights reserved in all countries. No part of this book may be reproduced in any form without written permission from the publisher. SportsZone™ is a trademark and logo of Abdo Publishing.

Printed in the United States of America, North Mankato, Minnesota
062017
092017

Cover Photo: Alex Gallardo/AP Images
Interior Photos: Alex Gallardo/AP Images, 1; Paul Sancya/AP Images, 4–5, 27; Seth Poppel/Yearbook Library, 7, 9; Tim Cowie/Icon Sportswire, 10; Brett Beier/Kalamazoo Gazette/AP Images, 12–13; Mary Ann Chastain/AP Images, 15; Duane Burleson/AP Images, 17; Seth Wenig/AP Images, 18–19; LM Otero/AP Images, 21; Marcio Jose Sanchez/AP Images, 23, 24–25; Sue Ogrocki/AP Images, 29

Editor: Todd Kortemeier
Series Designer: Craig Hinton

Publisher's Cataloging-in-Publication Data

Names: Smith, Brett, author.
Title: Stephen Curry : basketball MVP / by Brett Smith.
Other titles: Basketball MVP
Description: Minneapolis, MN : Abdo Publishing, 2018. | Series: Playmakers | Includes bibliographical references and index.
Identifiers: LCCN 2017930230 | ISBN 9781532111488 (lib. bdg.) | ISBN 9781680789331 (ebook)
Subjects: LCSH: Curry, Stephen, 1988- --Juvenile literature. | Basketball players--United States--Biography--Juvenile literature.
Classification: DDC 796.323 [B]--dc23
LC record available at http://lccn.loc.gov/2017930230

TABLE OF CONTENTS

Stephen Curry

CHAPTER 1

TOO SHORT, TOO SKINNY

Stephen Curry had never been here before. None of his Golden State Warriors teammates had made it this far either. It was Game 6 of the 2015 National Basketball Association (NBA) Finals. The Warriors had not won an NBA title since 1975. They faced LeBron James and the Cleveland Cavaliers. James was widely considered the best player in basketball.

Stephen Curry takes a shot in Game 6 of the 2015 NBA Finals.

But Curry and the Warriors were just one win away. In Game 6, the Warriors made 13 three-point shots. Curry had three of them. He tied for the team lead with 25 points. The Warriors beat James and the Cavaliers to become NBA champions.

The Warriors had won 67 games that season. Curry was the league's Most Valuable Player (MVP). He'd come a long way in nine years. When he was in high school, college teams didn't think he was good enough to play for them. No major program would offer him a scholarship. Now he was at the top of the sport.

Stephen Curry was born on March 14, 1988. His father was NBA player Dell Curry. Dell played with five different

Stephen, *right,* learned the game of basketball from his father, NBA player Dell Curry, *top.*

NBA teams in a 16-year career. Most of his career was spent in Charlotte, North Carolina, with the Hornets. That's where Stephen grew up. Besides basketball, he also played football, baseball, and soccer.

But he fell in love with basketball. His grandpa Jack's house had a hoop on an old light pole. It sat above an unpaved driveway. The ground was filled with loose rocks and tire tracks. It was the same hoop where Dell learned to shoot. A missed basket meant chasing the ball down the driveway. Both Dell and Stephen learned the importance of making every shot.

Stephen's favorite NBA player growing up was Muggsy Bogues. Bogues was the shortest player in NBA history. He stood only 5 feet 3 inches tall. Bogues played in the NBA for 14 years. He and Dell Curry were teammates in Charlotte.

Dell's NBA career ended in 2002. He started working on helping Stephen with his jump shot. It later became the best in basketball. Stephen was only about 5 feet 6 inches tall and

Stephen as a high school senior in 2005

125 pounds as a high school freshman. Physical strength was not his game. He would have to become a great shooter to make it to the NBA.

Stephen chose uniform No. 30 at Davidson, the same number his father wore in the NBA.

As a kid, even the smallest jersey looked three sizes too big on Stephen. But he was a hard worker. He was often the first to arrive at practice. And he was often the last to leave. The coaches at the Charlotte Christian School quickly realized something. They needed to build their program around Stephen. He became the Knights' team leader.

Stephen scored more than 1,400 points during his high school career. He averaged 18 points per game. It was a school record.

As a senior, he made 48 percent of his three-pointers. The Knights were runners-up at the state tournament. Stephen had impressive statistics. But he still received no scholarship offers from major college programs. He wanted to attend Virginia Tech. That was where his father had played. Dell was a member of the school's hall of fame.

But Virginia Tech only offered Stephen a spot as a walk-on player. That meant he might not even make the team. Stephen had grown to more than 6 feet tall and 160 pounds by then. But that was still considered too short and too skinny by major schools. Duke was one of the schools that turned him down. Duke coach Mike Krzyzewski later said that overlooking Stephen was a mistake.

Stephen did receive three scholarship offers. They were all to smaller schools. He chose Davidson College. Located in Davidson, North Carolina, it had less than 2,000 students. The Wildcats had not won a game in the national tournament since 1969. But then Stephen Curry showed up.

Stephen Curry

CHAPTER 2

ONE COOL CAT

Many people in North Carolina knew Dell Curry. But Stephen Curry was still a mystery to most fans. He came from a small high school and went to a small college. He wasn't thought of as a top NBA prospect like Kevin Durant from the University of Texas. And Curry's first game as a Wildcat was not very good.

Davidson won. And Curry scored 15 points. But he committed 13 turnovers. Coach Bob McKillop

Curry, *center*, goes up for a shot in a 2007 game with Davidson College.

didn't give up on him. Curry got a chance in the next game to show what he could do. The Wildcats faced the powerful University of Michigan. Curry scored 32 points and had nine rebounds. Even better, he had only three turnovers.

Curry had never dunked a basketball in a game until his freshman year at Davidson.

Curry finished the season second only to Durant among top-scoring freshmen. Curry played in all 34 games. He averaged 21.5 points per game. Davidson won the Southern Conference title. And Curry started getting noticed by NBA scouts.

He found the national spotlight at the end of his sophomore season. Davidson made the national tournament

Curry celebrates Davidson winning the 2007 Southern Conference tournament.

after the 2007–08 season. It hadn't won a game there in nearly 40 years. The Wildcats were ranked as a 10th seed. They needed an upset in their first game just to advance.

Curry was late for his first Davidson practice. He was kicked out of the gym as punishment. He never showed up late again.

They did a lot more than that. Curry and the Wildcats beat three of the top teams in the region. Gonzaga, Georgetown, and Wisconsin all fell to Davidson. In the Elite Eight, the Wildcats nearly knocked off No. 1 seed Kansas. But they lost by two. Kansas went on to win the national title.

Curry could have left for the NBA after his sophomore year. But he chose to stay in school. He played for Davidson for one more season.

Curry led the nation with 28.6 points per game in 2008–09. But Davidson didn't make it to the tournament. In three seasons

Curry walks off the court in disappointment after Davidson lost to Kansas in the 2008 national tournament.

he scored 2,635 points. That was a Davidson record. Curry decided he was going to turn pro. He entered the 2009 NBA Draft. With the seventh pick, the Warriors selected Curry. The kid who was too short and too skinny was going to the NBA.

Stephen Curry

CHAPTER 3

STRONG PROMISE, WEAK ANKLES

When Stephen Curry arrived in Oakland, California, home of the Warriors, he was 21 years old. He was 6 feet 3 inches tall and weighed 180 pounds. His height was average for a point guard. But he was too short to be an NBA shooting guard. Curry wasn't big or powerful like some players. But the Warriors coaches knew he could make good decisions. His rookie contract was worth nearly $13 million over four years.

Curry is congratulated by NBA commissioner David Stern after being drafted by the Golden State Warriors.

Curry's first two seasons as a pro were good. He averaged 17.5 points, 5.9 assists, and 1.9 steals per game as a rookie. It was a promising start to his career. Curry finished runner-up for the 2009–10 NBA Rookie of the Year Award.

During his second season, Curry missed eight games due to ankle injuries. He needed surgery on his right ankle after the season. The ankle was repaired and strengthened. The Warriors signed Klay Thompson in the same offseason. Thompson and Curry later became known as the "Splash Brothers." They had the ability to make difficult shots, especially three-pointers.

The ankle problems returned in 2011–12. Curry averaged just 14.7 points per game. It was his lowest total as an NBA

Curry shoots while competing at the NBA three-point contest in 2010.

player to that point. Curry's ankle injuries put his career in doubt. He wanted a second opinion. He had another surgeon take a look. It turned out that Curry's ankles were not that bad. They could be repaired. It was a simple operation. And the recovery time would be quick. He could start practicing again in three months.

Curry married his wife Ayesha in 2011. They have two daughters together. Riley was born in 2012 and Ryan followed in 2015.

Curry and his family were still concerned. The surgery might not be enough to save his career. But he didn't give up. When he was able, he spent a lot of time in the gym. He lifted weights to build muscle. He added on 10 pounds. Curry weighed 190 pounds when the next season tipped off. He also added strength. When he started training, he could only deadlift approximately 200 pounds (90.7 kg). By the time the season started, he could lift 400 pounds (181.4 kg).

"I Can do all things..."

Curry often writes inspirational messages on his shoes, like on this pair in 2012.

In 2012–13, he played in 78 games. He made 272 three-pointers. That was an all-time NBA record for a single season. The Warriors rewarded his great play. Curry signed a new contract for four years and $44 million. The Warriors made it to the second round of the playoffs. They lost to the San Antonio Spurs. But Curry's career was back on track.

Stephen Curry

CHAPTER 4

IMPOSSIBLY GOOD

I n 2014 the Warriors got a new coach. Steve Kerr was the fourth coach of Stephen Curry's NBA career. Like Curry and Klay Thompson, Kerr was also once an excellent three-point shooter. He played 15 NBA seasons. Most of them were with the Chicago Bulls.

Kerr developed a unique offensive strategy. His goal was to put the skills of his two best players

Curry celebrates after hitting a shot in the 2014 playoffs.

to use. That season Curry broke his own NBA record of most three-pointers in a season with 286. Thompson made 239.

Curry was already one of the best shooters in NBA history. One secret to his success is how quickly he moves. Curry can get in his shooting position in three-tenths of a second. That's about the amount of time it takes to blink your eyes. Curry can also release a shot in four-tenths of a second.

Curry was named the league MVP after the season. And the Warriors won their first championship in 40 years. They beat the Cleveland Cavaliers in six games. Curry led the Warriors in points per game with 26. He, Andre Iguodala, and Thompson hit more threes than the entire Cavaliers team. They celebrated back in Oakland with a parade and more than 100,000 fans.

Former President Barack Obama is also a big basketball fan. He called Curry the best shooter he had ever seen.

Curry, *left*, and teammate Andre Iguodala celebrate with the Larry O'Brien Trophy after winning the 2015 NBA Finals.

Curry was MVP and NBA champion. But in 2015–16, he and the Warriors were even better. Golden State started the season with 24 wins in a row. The previous NBA record was 15. The Warriors also went 73–9. That win total was another record. And Curry's three-point shooting only got better.

Once again, Curry topped his old record. But this time he shattered it. He hit 402 three-pointers. Thompson hit 276.

That would have been a record before Curry came along.
Curry won the NBA MVP Award again. Every voter chose Curry
for the award. Nobody else in NBA history had gotten every
single vote.

Curry's younger brother is also an NBA player. Seth Curry went
undrafted in 2013. But by 2016–17, he'd earned a part-time role on
the Dallas Mavericks.

The playoffs were tough for Curry and the Warriors. He hurt
his right knee in the first round. The injury kept him out until
the second round of the playoffs. But the Warriors overcame
it to make the NBA Finals again. They had a rematch with
the Cavaliers.

This time the Cavaliers got revenge. The Warriors won
three of the first four games, but Cleveland won the last three
to take the title. Curry missed a long three-pointer that could
have tied the final game in the last minute.

Curry signs autographs for fans before a 2017 game.

But Golden State got the last laugh. In 2016–17 Curry and new teammate Kevin Durant led the Warriors on tear. They posted the best record in the Western Conference. Then they lost just one game in four playoff series, beating the Cavaliers in five games to win their second title in three years. Some might consider Curry the best point guard in the NBA. He's certainly been one of the most successful.

FUN FACTS AND QUOTES

- Stephen Curry does a lot of charity work. Since he was in college, Curry has helped with the United Nations Foundation's Nothing But Nets program. This campaign works to provide mosquito nets to people in Africa.

- Curry's mom, Sonya, was also an athlete. She played volleyball for Virginia Tech.

- Curry's favorite childhood memory was when he got onstage with hip-hop group Kriss Kross.

- Curry first met NBA star Kevin Durant at a youth basketball event when he was 10 years old. In 2016, they became teammates on the Golden State Warriors.

- Curry loves golfing, and he's very good at it. He once played a round of golf with President Barack Obama.

- "Every time I rise up, I have confidence that I'm going to make it." —Curry on how he knows what a good shot is

WEBSITES

To learn more about Playmakers, visit **abdobooklinks.com**. These links are routinely monitored and updated to provide the most current information available.

GLOSSARY

assist

When a player helps another player score by passing the ball.

contract

An agreement to play for a certain team.

deadlift

An exercise that involves picking up a weight, lifting it up to the hips, and setting it back down.

freshman

A first-year student in high school or college.

offseason

The time of year when there are no games.

point guard

The player who leads the team when it has the ball and is trying to score.

prospect

An athlete likely to succeed at the professional level.

rebound

To catch the ball after a shot has been missed.

rookie

A first-year player.

scholarship

Money given to a student to pay for education expenses, sometimes in exchange for playing sports.

sophomore

A second-year student in high school or college.

steal

To take the ball from a player on the other team.

turnover

When a team or a player loses the ball to the other team because of a mistake.

walk-on

A player on a college team who does not receive a scholarship for participating.

INDEX

FURTHER RESOURCES

Campbell, Dave. *Stephen Curry*. Minneapolis, MN: Abdo Publishing, 2017.

Editors of *Sports Illustrated Kids* Magazine. *Sports Illustrated Kids Big Book of Who Basketball*. New York: Time Home Entertainment, 2015.

Schaller, Bob with Dave Harnish. *The Everything Kids' Basketball Book: The All-Time Greats, Legendary Teams, Today's Superstars—and Tips on Playing Like a Pro*. Avon, MA: Adams Media, 2015.